Effective Learning

Also available in the Ideas in Action Series

Effective Learning

Gavin Reid and Shannon Green

Ideas in Action

Illustrated by Tessa Lee

continuum

Continuum International Publishing Group

The Tower Building   80 Maiden Lane
11 York Road   Suite 704
London, SE1 7NX   New York, NY 10038

www.continuumbooks.com

British Library Cataloguing-in-Publication Data
A catalogue record for this book is available from the British Library.

ISBN: 1847065325 (paperback)

Library of Congress Cataloging-in-Publication Data
Reid, Gavin, 1950
Effective learning / Gavin Reid and Shannon Green.
    p. cm. – (Ideas in action)
ISBN 978-1-84706-532-2 (pbk.)
1. Effective teaching. 2. Learning. 3. Motivation in education.
I. Green, Shannon. II. Title. III. Series.

LB1025.3.R444 2009
371.102–dc22   2009006448

Typeset by Newgen Imaging Systems Pvt Ltd, Chennai, India
Printed and bound in Great Britain by Athenaeum Press Ltd.

Contents

About the authors and illustrator

Authors

Gavin Reid is the author of 23 books on teaching and learning. Formerly a senior lecturer, University of Edinburgh, he is now consultant to the Centre for Child Evaluation and Teaching in Kuwait, Red Rose School in the UK, the charity ASK in Geneva and has been visiting professor at the University of British Columbia in Vancouver, Canada.

Shannon Green holds a degree from Simon Fraser University in British Columbia and a post-graduate diploma in Difficulties in Literacy Development from the Open University in the UK. She is an experienced international trainer in literacy and learning and is the founder and director of a learning centre in Canada.

Illustrator

Tessa Lee is a freelance artist living on a farm in Alberta, Canada.

Introduction

This book is intended to provide the busy teacher with ideas for stimulating effective learning in the classroom. Focusing on how students learn and how to make learning more effective is particularly important in view of the heavy emphasis often given to curriculum content. It is perhaps too easy to become totally absorbed in ensuring that every part of the curriculum is taught at the right time. This in itself can put considerable pressures on teachers. Often they simply do not have time to reflect on how the curriculum should be delivered and more importantly the actual learning experiences students are gaining from education. Are these experiences meaningful? Can they be utilized for future learning? Do they make the student a more efficient and effective learner?

These are important questions that every teacher needs to consider, plan for and reflect on in terms of their own practice. Yet, often, 'learning' is not given a high priority – results are often seen as more important. Many students can perform and obtain good results, but that itself may be insufficient to make them effective learners. Often the distinction between performance and learning is blurred and many students have difficulty reflecting on how they can learn to become better learners. This is one of the key themes of this book – to help students develop independent learning skills so that they can become self-sufficient in learning at school and at home, and importantly beyond school.

In addition to encouraging teachers to reflect on the need to develop students' learning skills, this book also provides ready made examples that can immediately be applied to classroom learning. The 'idea' part of the book focuses on the reflection and justifies the importance of the idea while the 'action' part of the book provides tried and tested examples that can be used in the classroom.

We also see effective learning as not only a teacher's responsibility but also the concern of the whole school. It is important that everyone, including the school management, should be involved in attempting to make the school an exciting and stimulating learning environment. The final section of the book emphasizes that point. We have also considered the teachers perspective and have referred to ideas for reducing stress in the school. We feel a school that is immersed in, and prioritizes 'effective learning' is not only a successful school, but also a happy one.

1

Identifying and dealing with the barriers to learning

Layout of the classroom

The learning environment is important for effective learning. It is too easy to overlook this as other areas of learning may seem more urgent and more important.

Yet, some learners may be underperforming because they cannot concentrate, or may not feel relaxed with the classroom layout. For some, the environment can be stifling and restricting yet for others the same environment can be seen as secure and structured giving them the security and support they need when learning. Some of the factors that can be considered when you are planning the learning environment include:

- layout – the organization of classroom furniture

- the design of chairs and desks

- the position of teacher's desk in relation to the students

- the arrangement of the students' desks

- the flexibility in being able to move and adjust the layout of the classroom

- location of the classroom in relation to other classrooms in the school

- colour and shape of the room

- amount of light and

- amount of available space.

Consider the barriers that can prevent students from succeeding. These can be wide ranging – classroom environment, the task, memory, pace of work and understanding. It is a good idea to individualize the barriers by observing the student during learning.

Some types of learners, particularly auditory learners, will prefer desks to be in a conventional layout and will prefer sitting in an upright chair when learning. Others – particularly global, right brained learners – will prefer an informal classroom design and may even prefer to sit on a cushion on the floor rather than an upright chair. It is important to be flexible in the arrangement and the design of a classroom. This would mean that a number of different preferences can be accommodated. Ideally, the design should not be fixed and there should be scope for adaptations depending on the preferences of the current students in the class.

Before changing the layout of your classroom give consideration to the kinds of classroom environment you want to create – for example, highly structured environment with clear rules and routine to a very informal environment with considerable amount of freedom on the part of the students to move around and select learning materials. Some points you may want to consider are:

- the level of predictability

- the type of routine you want to impose

- class rules and the students' awareness of class rules

- the extent of freedom to move around the classroom

- how easy it is to locate items

- how stimulating is the environment.

- arrangement of the students desks – rows, groups, pairs, horseshoe shape and the position of the teacher's desk

When organizing the classroom I need to consider the following:

Factors

Desk layout

- are the desks individually placed, in pairs or grouped together
- is there desk space for individual work as well as a central work table

Wall displays

- Is there space for children to display own work themselves
- Are they informative, decorative, inspirational and current?

Space

- Are all the corner's used purposefully –eg reading corner, craft corner, reference corner etc.

Sound

- Is there music in the classroom – soft background music can help children work more effectively.

Light

- Are there different types of lights – table lamps as well as the main lights

Group dynamics

- How are the groups arranged – it is worthwhile experimenting with different types of groups.

Potential stress factors

avoid

- children being isolated from others
- too many classroom rules

encourage

- music, discussion, working together

Use scaffolds

You can't know a man until you have walked two moons in his moccasins.

Anon

Scaffolds are bridges that help to connect the learner with the task. They are essentially supports and it is important to select appropriate supports at the right level for the individual student. The term 'Zone of Proximal Development' (ZPD) is useful in this respect. Vygotsky (1978) suggested that there can be a significant difference, at any stage in learning, between what a learner can achieve unaided, compared to the situation where there is an instructor/teacher present and interacting with the learner. Vygotsky suggested that at any moment there are skills that are attainable, given the learner's current knowledge at that time, but these skills may not be accessible because the learner is not at a stage of preparedness to understand/absorb/implement these new skills. The set of skills that are currently attainable according to Vygotsky can be described as the 'Zone of Proximal Development' (ZPD). This means that one of the key aspects of effective teaching is to ensure that the learner is presented with tasks within his/her ZPD.

For teachers, the crucial question is how can a child's ZPD be identified and utilized effectively so that new information can be absorbed and then located within the ZPD. One of the starting points is to ensure that learners are introduced to the task so that they have a clear understanding of what the task is about (the purpose). Importantly, the teacher needs to be aware of the learner's previous knowledge within the area to be tackled (existing skills and knowledge). One way to obtain this is through the procedure called scaffolding. The process of scaffolding is like a series of steps that help the learner reach the ZPD needed in order to tackle the task effectively.

Each step will help the learner accommodate to the new learning experience. It is important to decide when to remove the scaffold – removing it too soon might result in failure; however, keeping the scaffold in place can result in an over dependency on the teacher/instructor. This is an important decision and is as important as deciding what type of scaffolds should be used.

In order to create appropriate scaffolding, it is important to have an understanding of the learner's previous knowledge and current skills such as: reading level, ability to locate informational text and background knowledge related to the topic. Once this information is known, the teacher can begin to create appropriate materials to support the topic the student is working on. These may include developing background knowledge or related information through group work, teacher questioning and field work followed by discussion to ensure that learning has taken place. A reciprocal question and answer technique with the student can be useful to ensure that the student has the same understanding of the task and related concepts as the teacher. The important point in relation to scaffolding is the language of the shared communication. Essentially, scaffolding involves a more skilled individual trying to impart knowledge to a less skilled person through the use of language exchange. The idea is to arrive at a shared understanding through the use of language. This is why Vygotsky suggested that the role of language is crucial to learning and to cognitive development. At the same time Vygotsky emphasized the role of the mediator (the teacher). The interaction between the teacher and the student is very important and this is an essential part of using scaffolds to identify the student's ZPD and develop the student's learning skills.

Make a list of the scaffolds you might use for the following teaching situations

- riding a bike
- learning letter sounds
- reading a book
- writing an essay
- learning to swim
- learning to skate
- giving a talk in public.

Information Processing

It is important to view each learner as an individual. Cognitive theory can be helpful as it relates to the role of information processing and the areas involved in processing such as memory, organization and the cognitive connections a learner makes when processing information. It can be argued that, to a great extent, effectiveness of learning can depend on the ability and skills the learner has in making these cognitive connections.

When a student is able to make connections during learning it is usually an indicator that he/she has a good understanding of the learning process. Being able to make connections makes learning meaningful and helps to develop an understanding of concepts and the 'ideas' that underpin the new learning. An effective learner can make these connections. The main area for making connections is between previous learning and new learning. Questions the learner could consider are: is there anything about the new learning that is familiar? How can I use this information to help with the new learning? Asking these questions will help learners connect between the previous learning and new learning and make learning more efficient.

Yet, many learners often fail to make these connections and this means that almost any learning activity becomes a totally new piece of learning. Often learners do not realize how they can make learning easier by utilizing the strategies and skills they used in prior learning.

The learning process involves input, cognition (thinking) and output. Some learners can experience challenges at all of these stages and therefore it might be useful to view these separately. For example are they actually taking in the information (input), are they able to understand it(cognition), are they able to demonstrate competence (output). It is good practice to get the student to look at his/ her strategies during each of these stages. It also helps the student to see learning as a process rather than facts that have to be learnt.

When tackling a learning activity, give the student a process to make learning more efficient. For example, if the question relates to reasons for the popularity of Shakespeare in seventeenth-century England the process might be as follows:

a. Resources – library, internet and group discussion – note the order in which materials are accessed. Some learners prefer to do the discussion first to get a better understanding of the question. Once they have this they may narrow it down by going to the library and then they will have a better idea of what to locate in the internet.

b. Culture – look for information on the culture in seventeenth-century England: poverty, pastimes, living accommodation.

c. Politics – what was the political situation like?

d. Entertainment – how was it viewed and what types were enjoyed/ available?

e. Other authors at the time.

f. Link these together and suggest three main reasons for the popularity of Shakespeare.

It is important to note this process as the same process can often be used in other questions on history, geography and English. It is also important to ask students to reflect on how they tackled the question and, importantly, how they may make the process more efficient.

This process can help to develop a structure for learning and this will make it easier for the learner to make connections between different areas of learning and become more aware of learning as a process and, importantly, the barriers and challenges they experience. Many students do not realize that the strategies and procedures they use in, for example, science can also be used in other subjects. This aspect is really related to study skills and it is never too early to introduce study skills to children. Teaching children 'how to learn' is just as important as the 'what to learn' question. This is also a good opportunity to introduce the need to use different parts of the brain for learning and how the brain can become more efficient when you use it for different areas of learning. You can even engage the student in some practical activities such as making up a song about learning or doing an annotated drawing.

2 Learning to learn

Introduce a metacognitive cycle

The term metacognition refers to the abilities of the learner to maximize his/her learning potential. Metacognition means 'thinking about thinking'. The extent to which learners are aware of the thinking and learning processes they are using will have an impact on the learning outcome. Four important aspects of this relate to:

- how learners can **direct** their learning

- how they can **monitor** the learning experience

- how they can **assess** the results of their learning and evaluate the learning experience, and

- the extent to which they are able to **transfer** this learning/knowledge to a new learning situation.

The learning experience is often overlooked, yet it is extremely important. The learning experience refers to how learners feel about the learning situation and how they can use the resources and their previous knowledge to understand and access the material/skills that are being taught.

Learners who have a high degree of metacognitive awareness

- are usually efficient and successful learners

- have some appreciation of their own learning style since this knowledge can help to make learning more efficient

- would ask themselves how they arrived at a particular response

- would be able to understand the information they needed to obtain that response

Two key areas in learning to learn are metacognition and learning styles. Metacognition is the ability to know how to tackle a task and learning styles relates to all aspects of the learning experience. These can make learning more effective.

Using the metacognitive cycle outlined here will take the student through the learning process and will try to provide the student with insights on effective learning as well as providing the student with some ownership over his/her own learning. This is more appropriate for students further up the school, but with teacher input it can also work with younger students.

1. Questioning – ask yourself about new information – why/how is it relevant? What do I need to know? Do I understand it?

2. Clarify – ask yourself questions to clarify any concepts or vocabulary.

3. Understanding – ensure that you have a good understanding of the new information, as this will help you to remember it and use it much later.

4. Monitor – ask yourself if you are on the right track. How do I know?

5. Assess – Try to assess your own performance in whatever you are doing. Ask yourself – have I answered the question that was being asked? What else might I have done?

Throughout this process you can get the student to think aloud as this can help the teacher find out how the student is actually engaging with the task. It also helps the student too as often students are unaware of their own learning processes. During this process the teacher should be able to ask questions such as: Can you describe the task itself? Why are you doing this? How does this relate to the task? How did you arrive at this? Do you understand the relevance of the task?

It is important that the student is able to reflect afterwards on how they did the task. The teacher should then discuss with them if the process was successful, how it could have been more efficient and what the student might want to do next time.

- would be aware of which strategies were successful and which were not

- would know how they could use specific strategies to tackle future problems.

Some students, even those who obtain a correct response, are often unsure how they obtained the actual response. It is important to help learners become aware of the processes they are using and, importantly, why they elected to use a particular approach.

Develop independent learning

What we are suggesting in this chapter is that independent learning is essential for effective learning. We are also indicating that students need to know the right questions to ask before and during the learning process. But the important point is that not only do they need to know the right questions to ask but they also need to know how to answer them! To do this they need to have an understanding of the task – if they do not, they need to know how to obtain that understanding. For example, which books or websites to refer to and which questions they need answering. This investigation of finding out what to do and how to tackle a question is important. Students would usually be inclined to rely on the teacher to provide this information. We need to look for ways of encouraging students to do this on their own. This can be done by devising a checklist of available resources for the students, and having them decide which ones would be useful for the task they are working on. In other words, the teacher could provide a structured work plan with some spaces so that there is a degree of autonomy but the students are not left totally on their own. There could also be some guidance and discussion so that the students can come up with questions they need to answer before they can complete the task.

It is too easy for students to become dependent on a teacher or even on other students in the class. Some students find it difficult to break this dependency, particularly students who have any kind of learning difficulties. It is important, therefore, to try to empower learners by giving them the confidence, opportunity and resources to work out their problems themselves – otherwise teaching and learning can become prescriptive, repetitive and may not stimulate the student.

A part of the classroom can be identified as a 'no hands up zone'. This means that when the student enters this area they know that they will not be allowed to ask questions. Structured study plans could be provided for the student to begin with to help them tackle the questions without prompts from the teacher. It is possible for two or more students to enter this area together to collaborate with each other.

The no hands up zone can also be a fun type of activity for the student and some might even see it as a reward. Get the children to draw posters showing it is a no hands up zone and why it is a no hands up zone.

The emphasis is on thinking skills and children working things out themselves; therefore, emphasis could be made on the fact that questions are not permitted while in 'the zone'.

Help students identify their learning style

Learning styles is an area that does attract some controversy. The critics of learning styles argue that it is impossible and misleading to identify students with a particular learning style and they raise doubts on whether the instruments that are currently available actually do measure learning style. There has been criticism on the lack of validity and reliability. In this section, we are seeing learning styles not as a precise science but as a guide for both the teacher and the learner. We would prefer to use the term learning preferences as it suggests a more flexible approach to learning and does not seem to be as fixed as the idea of a learning style.

We are, therefore, suggesting that for classroom and teaching purposes it is beneficial to use some form of identification for learning 'preferences', even if it may not be a precise, or infallible measure of ones learning style. This should be seen as a guide. Most of the instruments assessing learning style are based on self-report and are essentially questionnaires. While questionnaire and self-report instruments can be useful, they only provide a guide and need to be supplemented with other means of assessment such as observation.

It is also important to view learning styles or learning preferences in a comprehensive way. That means there needs to be a focus on:

- the cognitive area – that is, how students process information

- social learning – whether they prefer to learn on their own or with others

- environmental preferences – classroom layout, desks, light and sound in the learning environment – all can have some impact

- intrapersonal/metacogntive style – this relates to the degree to which the learners are aware of their style and of how to learn.

Asking students the following questions will provide a quick learning styles summary. For younger children you can read the questions out to them or find pictures to describe the different situations in the questions. Some students may need some explanation for each of the questions. It is important to consult with the student over the responses. We have used the term responses rather than results as this indicates that there is no right or wrong answer.

- Do you prefer to work when it is quiet – does background noise disturb you?

- Do you like to talk with people while you are working or work quietly by yourself?

- Do you like to listen to music while you are working?

- Do you prefer to work with a dim table light or bright lights?

- Do you like to work with something warm on such as a sweater or fleece, or do you prefer to be cool?

- Do you like a lot of space in the classroom?

- Do you prefer learning through listening to someone?

- Do you like to make or do something when you are learning?

- Do you like to move around when you are working on something?

- Do you prefer to take time to think about something before doing it or do you want to do it now?

From the responses to these questions you will obtain some idea of the student's cognitive preferences, for example, visual, auditory, kinaesthetic and also their environmental preferences – space, sound, light etc. This information can be used as a starting guide, and through observation (see next page) and questioning you can find out more information about their preferences. This should help you in your planning and in the acquisition and allocation of resources.

Identifying learning styles through observation

There are many different types of instruments that can be used in observation. Some of these involve the use of a checklist that can monitor the student's style, motivation, social skills and listening and comprehension skills or indeed almost any area of learning. This type of checklist, however, may be restrictive as it may not apply to your classroom and may not focus on the student's learning style.

Ideally, observation should be diagnostic, flexible and adaptable. Furthermore, it should take place in a natural setting such as the classroom. Observation can be diagnostic because they can provide on-going opportunities to analyse student responses in different learning situations. These responses can be noted and a learning styles profile developed for the student.

An observational framework rather than a checklist may be more helpful. A framework can be adaptable and can be customized for different ages, classrooms and learning situations. It is important to observe the student in the learning situation. This is a more natural setting and you can note the students' social behaviours, academic performance and study habits across a range of tasks which provide information on the student's learning style.

By using a framework, it is also possible to be interactive – so, you are not only observing the student, but you are also interacting with him/her. This can make observations more illuminating as it can facilitate asking metacognitive questions about the learning process. (This is also dealt with in this chapter.) These questions can include asking students how they tackled a particular learning task and asking why they did this. This can provide insights into the student's awareness of learning and can also give some insights into the students' learning style which will also be covered in the next chapter.

Develop a framework for observation to collect information on the student's preferences for learning. The framework below offers a suggestion of how this can be developed.

- Motivation – What topics, tasks and activities interest the student? What kinds of prompting and cueing seem to increase motivation?

- Persistence – Does the student stick with a task until completion without breaks? Are frequent breaks necessary when working on difficult tasks?

- Responsibility – To what extent does the student take responsibility for his/her own learning? Does the student attribute successes and failures to self or others?

- Structure – Are the student's personal effects (desk, clothing, materials) well organized or cluttered? How does the child respond to someone imposing organizational structure on him or her? When provided with specific, detailed guidelines for task completion, does the student faithfully follow them, or work around them?

- Modality preference – What type of instructions – written, oral, visual or experiential – Does the student understand most readily?

- Impulsive versus reflective – Are the student's responses rapid and spontaneous or delayed and reflective?

- Mobility – Does the student move around the class frequently or fidgets when seated?

- Time of day – During which time of the day is the child most alert?

- Sound – Does the student seek out places to work which are particularly quiet?

- Light – Does the student like to work in dimly lit areas or do they say that the light is too bright?

- Furniture design – When given a choice, does the child sit on the floor, lie down or sit in a straight chair to read?

- attention – does the student attend better when listening or doing something, working on his/her own or with a group

Recognize the importance of attribution theory

Attribution theory suggests that one of the most important motivating factors in people's lives is the sense they make of their perceived successes and failures. The theory suggests that people can attribute their actions – successes and failures – to either internal reasons, that is, 'due to the individual'; or external reasons, that is, 'due to external forces or influences'. They may also see some outcomes as changeable or fixed and controllable or uncontrollable.

This means that the student can attribute his/her success to the teacher or to another member of the group or to a book or resource he/she was using. If students are experiencing a difficulty with a task, for example, a maths problem, they may see the outcome as **fixed** and out of their control and decide that they cannot do maths and give up. Attribution theory, therefore, relates to the extent the student attributes success to him/herself or to some other factor.

Some students may perceive a difficulty they are experiencing as being due to limited intelligence (internal locus) or to poor teaching (external locus). They may see themselves as capable of developing their learning skills by hard work (controllable), or they may see themselves as simply unable to learn however hard they try (uncontrollable). This latter example is often called learned helplessness and can be a destructive influence in the student's self-esteem. The idea is to try to get the student to attribute success to him/herself. That would mean they have control over the task and over their learning. It also means that if they fail they can do something about it – the answer is in their hands. This can pave the way for the development of self-esteem. It can also promote independent and more confident learning.

Get students to develop their own personal learning plan. This helps to give them ownership over the task and the learning that is taking place. This means they will, more likely, attribute the outcome to themselves rather than displace the responsibility on something else. It is important that they are giving guidance to themselves in working out their own personal learning plan and profile.

My Personal learning profile

My preferred learning style is _____

My preferred learning environment includes _____

When I am studying independently, I prefer to _____

My preferred way of making notes includes _____

My preferred revision techniques are _____

My preferred time of day is _____

I will need to review my learning plan every _____

After reviewing my plan, I propose the following changes _____

This can lead on to the student being able to develop their own final study plan for each activity they are working on.

My study plan		
Activity	**Things that help**	**Things to avoid**
Reading		
Spelling		
Creative writing		
Remembering		
Information		
Brainstorming		

The idea behind this is that students, by devising their own learning plan, are able to take control of the learning situation and therefore will be more likely to attribute the outcome of learning to their own efforts.

Stress proof the student

It is important to get the student in the right frame of mind for learning, and it is necessary to ensure that students realize that they need to prepare themselves for challenging learning. Although this may seem more appropriate for students further up the school, it is important that it is implemented when they are in the early stages so that they realize and appreciate the importance of relaxation and preparation for learning.

This again helps to pass the responsibility for learning to the student and helps them appreciate that they can influence the outcome. It is a good idea to introduce them to a range of different relaxation techniques, but it is best to keep it simple. This will mean that they can use the approach when they are on their own and at home.

Following is a list of ideas that will help with guiding students through relaxation.

Preparation

- Ensure that all items that may be distracting are out of sight.
- If relaxation is to take place in the classroom, ensure that the desks are cleared.
- Dim the lights as this will minimize distraction and aid visualization.
- If you are giving instructions, speak in a softer voice than usual.
- When coming out of the relaxation period increase the volume of your voice gradually.

Techniques

- Eyes are closed while listening to classical music.
- Visualization techniques – imagine a scene such as a beach or holiday destination.
- Free time – allowing time for favourite activity without any form of structure or demands.
- Exercises involving body flexing such as yoga and stretching.
- Introducing games and sports activities.
- Puzzles – word searches, colouring and other activities.

It is a good idea to get the student to think about his/her own preferred relaxation techniques. This indicates that the same technique may not work for everyone so it is okay to have your own preferred technique. You can reinforce this by getting students to make a chart and a timetable for relaxation.

My favourite relaxation techniques are: _____

My best time for relaxation is _____

Develop cooperative and collaborative learning

Students need to practise working collaboratively. For some students this may not be easy. But some tasks can be tackled more effectively if it is a product of group work. This helps students recognize not only their own strengths but also, importantly, recognize the strengths in others. This is essential for effective group work.

It is an idea to try to introduce group work from the 'supporting others' perspective. Each group member will have a responsibility to support one other member of the group. This underlines the fact that the group, although it is made up of individuals, needs to take on a group identity. This may not be easy but with practice each member of the group can become aware of the skills and the challenges of others in the group and it may be important to discuss this with the group before and after the task.

It is important to emphasize that the cohesion of the group is as important as the task they are embarking on. Some members of the group, particularly older students, may be familiar with reality TV shows that now increasingly feature groups of people – whether in a house, the jungle, beach or business venture – who have been thrown together and have to gel as a group. This might be a good analogy as the object of these shows is to identify those who can work for the group rather than for themselves.

Group dynamics is also an important factor and it is good to ensure that there is a mix of learning styles in the group and that you monitor how the group is working together. Perhaps one person is too dominant or some are left out altogether? Try to ensure that each member of the group has a role to play.

The students are all part of a television network station working on a TV news programme featuring live interviews. The stages they will need to consider are:

- Preparation: choose a range of topics to research.

- Props: identify background props and images for the interviews and reports.

- Responsibilities: each group member has to take on a role that could include reporters, researchers, anchor people, producers/directors, interviewees and any other role the group may wish to identify with. Visit a TV studio if this is possible.

- Programme: the students should set actual programme timings. There may also be 'breaking news' stories that are introduced by the producer.

- Plan a team-briefing meeting wherein one meeting is held before the programme and another is held after the programme to reflect on how it progressed. This is very important as the reflection meeting would also include pointers for future group work. The group should look at the good points of the exercise and discuss on how they may improve in the future.

3 Memory

Do not overload

For simplicity, memory can be divided into two main aspects, both of which are important for learning – short-term memory and long-term memory. Short-term memory, or working memory, as it is sometimes called, deals with the very short-term stimuli which is then processed and transferred to long-term memory. The process involves understanding, organization and storing information for retrieval. The degree of ease of retrieval depends on how well the student has understood and organized the information. It should be noted that memory is not synonymous with learning. Many students make this association and almost give up learning because they believe they have a poor memory. It is important to emphasize this point to students and also indicate that it is possible to improve memory. One of the key aspects of memory relates to how well the information is understood. It is important that the student spends time understanding rather than attempt to cram and memorize information without full understanding. If there is no real understanding, then the information will only be retained for a short period and may not be used appropriately. Understanding, therefore, is a key aspect of long-term memory.

Giving one piece of information at a time can be helpful, particularly for short-term memory. Short-term memory is an important part of the learning process because it signals the initial stage of the learning process and if information is not effectively processed in short-term memory then it will be lost and will not be processed into long-term memory and therefore it will not be as readily recalled. Attention is also an important factor in memory, particularly short-term memory. Many students will lose attention if too much information is being presented to them at the same time.

One way of assisting the student to attend and to process information in short-term memory is to present only one piece of information at a time. Many students are capable of holding more than one piece of information at a time and in this case more than one can be presented. The key point is – do not overload. This can be worked out on an individual basis in order to gauge the student's short-term memory capacity.

The student can keep a chart of information retained. For example, they may have a heading 'important points about this information' and then list the points.

I like doing memory strategies because I always forget.

Lisa (aged 10)

Prioritize

Students usually always have too much to learn – or so they might think! But feeling overburdened is common for students particularly as the curriculum appears to becoming more and more crammed and often students, even young students, have much more to learn than they have time for. Often they have to be selective and make choices. We are surrounded by choices and decisions everyday, and in everyday life it is necessary to prioritize. It is no different for students when they are studying.

They need to gain practice in doing this. When a student has a list of things to achieve, it can be difficult for him/her to decide what to do first and what is less important. This can apply to daily tasks as well as to specific areas of study. It is important that students are presented with dilemmas that requires decisions to be made and practise prioritizing the different tasks to be carried out.

Problem solving tasks can be helpful for this – this can be done by providing the student with dilemmas over how to spend money or how to spend their time.

Prioritizing actions can help to clear the mind of competing tasks to be carried out and this will allow the student to focus exclusively on the task in hand and not worry about the other things that have to be carried out.

It also helps with self-organization and this is important for effective learning. Prioritizing can therefore be a step towards thinking and learning independently. The popular 'to do list' types of activities can also help students to prioritize their work.

Remember – small steps can lead to giant leaps!

Help the student develop a daily or weekly priority schedule.

My weekly priority schedule is			
Day	**Task**	**Carried out**	**Comment**
Monday	Read chapter 1 of the novel study for English	Completed and reread twice with notes	Need to find out about the social conditions at the time the novel is set – nineteenth-century Europe
Tuesday			
Wednesday			
Thursday			
Friday			
Weekend			

This schedule can be used to keep track of progress as well as to help with prioritizing and forward planning. The comment section of the table can be used to identify any challenging aspects of learning and to suggest what else is needed to complete the task.

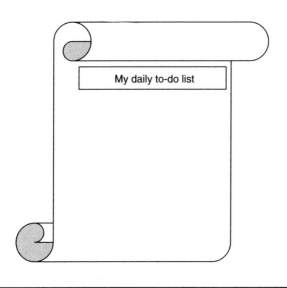

My daily to-do list

Organizing information

One of the reasons why some people have an effective memory is because they are able to organize the information at the time of learning and immediately afterwards. Many students concentrate on getting the information down on paper through note-taking and then at some later point they start to rearrange the information. This can be effective as the student is personalizing the information to make it more meaningful to him/her. But it can be more effective if students can organize the information at the time of learning. That is, as they are making the notes they should be arranging the information into some sort of meaningful manner. Not only is this a more efficient way to study, but it can also enhance comprehension.

Organizing the information at the time of learning can be easier for students if they use some sort of framework.

Framework for organization

Topic – Novel study	
Headings I can use for key points	
Why are these key points?	
Main themes – i.e. the general points	
Implications of each theme for the novel	
Background Political Social Economic	
Connections with other topics/subjects	
Prioritize information – most important to less important	

Student should use this chart not only to help with organization but also to monitor their progress. They should be able to use this as a template for a number of different topics.

The key information should be the same – that is, key points, main theme, identify headings, implications, any additional background information, connections with different areas and placing the information into a list that can be used to organize and assess the importance of each piece of information. This can also form the beginnings of a study plan.

Use headings and subheadings

Organization is important for memory – the key to organizing information is the ability to identify the general theme of the information and to arrange the information so that it can be understood and retained. Students have to learn all sorts of information and these units of learning may seem disparate and diverse to the student. This will make it more difficult to learn, to understand and to recall. The use of headings and subheadings can not only help to organize the information but also it can help to put the information into some kind of meaningful context. It should be possible for the student to go through pages of notes by just looking at the headings and subheadings and be able to understand the whole piece. Visuals can reinforce this – perhaps a visual for each heading as an aide memoire. This helps to personalize the information and this is crucial for retention and recall.

Reading other people's notes may not be too helpful – notes need to be personalized and that includes handouts from teachers. The students need to write down their own comments on the printed sheet. These comments should include what the student thinks the implications are. So, they can have the heading 'implications' in the margin and write the implications in a phrase next to each paragraph. It is important to practise using heading and subheadings.

Whether you think you can or think you can't you're probably right.

Henry Ford

Select a piece of text and identify some possible headings and subheadings.

Ideas for headings – each of the questions below will provide an idea for a heading or a subheading.

- Ask yourself – what is it about? (That will provide one heading.)
- Who is it about?
- Where does it take place?
- What do you know about the background?
- Is there anything unusual or different in the story?
- What will help me remember it?
- What are the implications?
- If I had 10 seconds to tell someone about it, what phrase would I use?

Example

Suggested headings are in brackets and bold. (Children's perception of reading.) It is worthwhile emphasizing that children's perception of reading is an important element in how successful and motivated they will be with reading. **(Motivation and reading.)** One of the most successful means of motivating children to read is to ensure that the reading material is age appropriate, culturally appropriate and of interest to the child.

It is good to provide opportunities for individual selection of books of the child's own choice.

(Strategies) This is one of the main aspects of paired reading. In this reading procedure it is crucial that the child chooses his/her own reading material.

Get students to keep on practising at making up headings for their notes.

Chunk

Chunking is an excellent strategy to organize information and to help with retention. It is interactive and personal – you decide what items should be chunked together. We might suggest a possible way of chunking information here but it may be different from the one you might choose. It is important that chunking is personalized, but some students may need a structure to help them. There are some items, however, that might be better going together. For example, if you are studying the Harry Potter books you might put information relating to the location, the characters and the school together. Giving students possible headings to help with chunking can be useful. Ideally, the items to be chunked together should be related in some way. This is where the organization comes in as the student has to actively think about the information and try to understand it at the time of learning so that it can be effectively chunked. This means that the student will need to interact with the learning and not just try to retain in through rote learning. That is why it is better to get students to put the information into chunks themselves rather than providing them with a list.

Chunking can be useful if the student is giving a talk to the rest of the class – it is a more efficient way of learning than writing down lists of items. Chunking can also help with making connections (which was) discussed earlier in this chapter. Essentially these are all part of the process of learners taking responsibility for their own learning. That is why it is best to get learners to practise doing their own chunking as it will be individual to them and by personalizing it in this way they are more likely to understand the information and retain it. The key to this strategy is practice.

Place all similar pieces of information into one group – for example, if you are studying the geography of a country, make a chunk of all the facts relating to climate. Then make a list of all items within that climate: rain, sun, effects, global warming etc. You should be able to chunk at least four items together. So, find at least four items that have a strong connection.

Try to make chunking fun – and personalize it as much as possible. The more personal it is to you, the easier it will be to remember. For example, in the diagram below, the student had to remember all the countries of Europe and their capitals. A list of some 26 countries can be formidable but by chunking the countries into geographical locations, the task will be a lot easier.

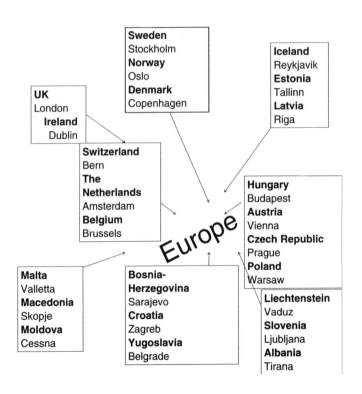

Make connections

You need to make connections all the time when learning. This makes learning meaningful and aids understanding and the development of concepts. An effective learner is one who is able to make these connections. The main connection is between previous learning and new learning. Questions learners need to consider are – is there anything about the new learning that is familiar? What is familiar and why? How did I tackle this before? Should I do the same again or can I improve on this? This will help learners connect between the previous and new learning and by asking themselves questions about how they tackled it previously, they can help to make learning more efficient.

Connections also help with understanding and can make learning more efficient. We should encourage learners to do this all the time by getting them to ask themselves questions such as those above, all the time, when they are tackling learning.

Making connections also helps with self-monitoring while the student is engaged in the task. This is essential in order for the students to take responsibility for their own learning. This means that students need to ask questions for themselves as they are learning. They need to know the questions to ask themselves such as: what have I to do here? How does this relate to what I already know? What else do I need to find out? These types of questions provide scope for self-reflection and provide evidence that the students are to take responsibility for their own learning and will be in a position to make the kind of connections needed for efficient learning.

Many students, particularly in secondary school, see learning within the parameters of the subject area. They often have difficulty in cross referencing between different subjects. In many cases similar words and concepts can occur but the student may not realize this unless it is explicitly pointed out by the teacher.

As indicated in the previous page many students will need to be shown how to make connections. This can be done by using a mind map or a spidergram. To begin with, provide examples of connections for different topics that can be readily connected such as: the weather chain, animal food chain, money chain.

Then move on to make connections with information within the same subject, such as: animals of the jungle, pets, garden plants, types of fruit and vegetables. For more advanced students you can suggest the link between social conditions and political change, workers oppression and social unrest.

You can then move to make connections with topics and events drawn from across the curriculum such as: history and English literature, geography and science, design technology and physics.

If you can make the connections fun filled and personalize them, then you will be more likely to remember them and remember the significance of each connection.

Mind maps are a good way to make connections because they present only relevant material in a clear and memorable form. Unlike linear text, mind maps show not just the facts but also the relationship between those facts giving the students a deeper understanding of the subject and thus helping the student to make connections.

Mind maps are a good way to use visuals, make connections and also to help with organization. Some advantages of mind maps are shown below.

- Mind maps can inspire interest in the students making them more receptive and cooperative in the classroom.

- Because mind maps tend to present only relevant material in a clear and memorable form, students tend to get better marks in examinations.

- Unlike linear text, mind maps show not just the facts but also the relation between those facts, thus giving the students a deeper understanding of the subject.

- The physical volume of notes is dramatically reduced.

Re-enact

Drama lessons have brought me 'out of my shell'.

David (aged 11)

Drama has helped me talk in front of people because I never used to have confidence but now I have become a lot more expressive.

Kelly (aged 13)

Learning should be active. The more active the learner; the more likely the information will be understood and retained. The activity could be in the form of discussion but it could also be in drama form and first person speech. This can be done more easily in some subjects such as history where first person and drama can be used to re-enact historical events.

Feelings of frustration can be quite common when children are learning something new and challenging. Even able students can experience these feelings. This can be demotivating and destructive. They may lead to anger and subsequent behavioural difficulties in the classroom. Drama can provide an outlet to prevent this. When the voices of children with dyslexia are heard and their views and feelings are understood, frustrations can be minimized.

Create simple improvizations from freeze-frames. Begin by asking the class to form simple freeze-frames in small groups, for example, photo album snaps. Ask the whole class to produce two large-scale freeze-frames of first day at school and end of term (facial expressions are important). Split the class into two large groups. Ask each group to create a photo freeze-frame from the members of the other group. Give each group until the count of ten to mould the opposite group into the picture and give the finished product a title. From the picture, each group must produce two minutes worth of improvization, either before or after the freeze.

Now you are ready to bring the freeze-frames to life. Get the students to relax and ask for volunteers to show their freeze-frames and role-play to the class. Ask each group to hold their freeze-frame, count down '3, 2, 1 GO!' After about 30 seconds say, 'and freeze'. This can be a fun activity and a number of different aspects of learning can result from this, as well as the fun and the peer interaction from collaboration.

Students may now feel more able to participate in role-play activities. Get students in groups of four and get them to talk about a memorable event that happened during the holidays. If nothing interesting happened tell them to invent something! Decide on a freeze-frame to start the drama. You are going to bring it to life for 30 seconds and use words this time. You have 3 minutes to practise it. The events can be quite commonplace (like going shopping with friends) or extraordinary incident (like witnessing an accident). This time they have to talk about what they are doing but they are still working in conjunction with their peer group.

Discuss

For some learners discussion is the only way in which they can retain and understand information. Discussion can make the information meaningful and can help the learner experiment with ideas and views. It is this experimentation that helps the learner extend their thinking and learning. For some learners discussion can be like thinking aloud. It is important that there are opportunities for discussion – it may be useful to actually timetable discussion time and split the class into smaller groups.

One of the good points about discussions is that it involves listening and reflecting as well as talking. This is a good exercise for many students as it enhances sharing of views and listening to other's opinions. It can be useful to provide the class with group tasks rather than individual tasks – even for assignments – as this would mean that they need to discuss the points and agree on a joint opinion. This has value for younger children as well as students further up the school.

Introduce discussion words such as: describe, compare, analyse, judge, provide. Indicate what each word means with examples and get them to try it out. Start with material that is very familiar to them to begin with and then move to more abstract and complex material.

Combine the benefits of drama with improvization by introducing some scenarios that they may be familiar with or even some that may not be known to them. The benefit of the latter is that it can help to inspire creativity. Ideally the students should work in pairs. The situations work best if the students get straight into them and avoid long discussions.

Possible scenarios for improvization

- Hairdresser and customer (after hair disaster)
- Photographer and awkward supermodel
- Two strangers on a train – one is smoking in a non-smoking compartment
- Suspect being interviewed by the police
- Boss giving employee the sack
- Door-to-door salesman and lonely pensioner
- Job interview
- Parent and teenager – teenager three hours late, parent waiting up
- Two cars meet, coming from opposite directions, down a narrow country lane. One belongs to a farmer, the other to a wealthy businessman – who moves first?
- Pupil sent to Head Teacher for bad behaviour.

The 5 R's – recognize, revise, review, recall and reflect

Students often remember the process better if you use acronyms such as that above.

- **Recognize** – identify your own preferred way of learning.

- **Revise** the information that is to be learnt. The important point is that this revision can take a number of different forms but will work more effectively if there is a revision plan and timetable.

- **Review** – this is important as it is the reviewing that consolidates memory and ensures understanding and retention in long-term memory. This will make it easier to remember.

- **Recall** – this also needs to be practised – simply the more you use a skill or piece of information the more easily it will be memorized and recalled in future use.

- **Reflect** – this can be done through the use of reflective questions such as why and how, and also through thinking and even thinking aloud. But reflection is important for effective learning and to help the learner become more efficient as a learner so they can use an effective strategy the next time they are learning something similar.

The important point about this process is that it provides a framework for the student that can be individualized and students can utilize their own individual strategies within the framework. This can be more effective than providing the student with a range of random memory strategies.

Take a sample of students' work and help them to use the 5 R's and how they can incorporate this into their study pattern.

Draw a board game with the 5 R's interspaced through the game – leave blanks for the student to show how he/she has used these.

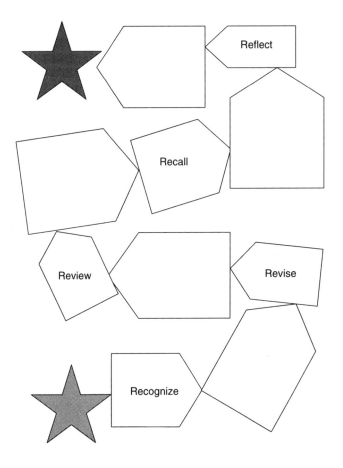

Motivation

Stimulate to motivate

Many of the techniques for effective learning are based on providing motivation and stimulation to ensure that students want to learn. There are a number of points to consider when developing motivation. These can included ensuring that:

- the task is related to the students' **interests**

- the student appreciates the **value** of the task

- the student can **achieve** the task

- **feedback** is available throughout the task and immediate feedback at the end

- the student is **emotionally** prepared for the task

- the student is **comfortable** in the learning environment.

Each of these points can represent good teaching practice. But it is important that each of the points be considered in relation to motivation. It is also important, therefore, to consider the individual characteristics of the student. This can be done from a pre-planning perspective. We need to find out the areas that interest the student and give the task some value by attaching some kind of motivational weighting to the task. The importance of the task has to be clear to the student but what is of greatest importance is that the task must be achievable. The student has to have a perception of success in that he or she is able to perceive the task as achievable. This can be a great motivator. It is also important to consider the student's needs from a holistic perspective. That means we need to ensure that students are emotionally ready for the task. Emotional factors can have an impact on motivation and these should be considered at all stages of learning.

Motivation is essential for effective learning, it is crucial to try to make motivation intrinsic so that learners become self-motivated. You can use extrinsic motivation such as rewards, but try to shift this to intrinsic motivation as soon as possible.

Make up a motivation checklist such as the one below, but you may want to contextualize it for your own work situation.

Motivation checklist

Interest	Task	Differentiation	Emotional factors
How students' interests have been considered?	How does the student's previous understanding enable him/her to complete the task?	Are there different forms of the task for the less able and the more able?	How do we know that the student will be able to tackle the learning in a positive frame of mind?
List points here			
1.			
2.			
3.			

Locus of control

The concept of locus of control is an important one for motivation. Locus of control can be internal or external and it is important to appreciate the role played by both in motivation.

An internal locus of control means that the student has accepted that he/she has responsibility for the outcome. This means that they will more likely attribute the success of an outcome to their own efforts. This is helpful for motivation.

An external locus of control means that he/she would shift the responsibility to some external influence. The student can then attribute success or (failure) to some external factor and this can prompt an 'opting out' of responsibility over the learning situation. It is important, therefore, that the student develops an internal locus of control and this will pave the way for accepting responsibility and developing independence.

Example
External locus of control

I failed my essay because . . . the teacher did not tell us what to do.

Internal locus of control

I failed my essay because . . . I did not study the relevant pieces of information.

Get the students to develop their own study plan including a list of things that will support them in studying and things that may interfere with their studying.

My study plan		
Activity	Things that help	Things to avoid
Reading		
Spelling		
Creative writing		
Remembering		
Information		
Brainstorming		

My favourite strategies

1.

2.

3.

4.

Make individual education plans motivating

When it is obvious that the goals cannot be reached, don't adjust the goals, adjust the action steps.

Confucius

The development of Individual Education Plans (IEPs) indicates that a degree of forward planning has been put into place. The range and nature of IEPs can, however, vary considerably. There is usually a focus on student outcomes, but it is important that motivation be kept in mind as the plan is unfolding. Are the activities motivating? How can they be made more motivating? What types of resources are motivating for the student? Some key points that can be kept in mind include:

- The need for formative reflection – that is, to look ahead and be proactive rather than merely summative reporting – that is, recording what has happened or will happen.

- The need for student and parent involvement in addition to the school-based team.

- The importance of using a variety of instructions.

- The importance of peer involvement.

- The need to recognize the students' individual learning preferences.

- Are the resources multi-sensory?

- Are they accessible and stimulating?

- Is there inbuilt monitoring of the student for reviewing progression – this is necessary for motivation.

IEPs should offer a means of checking and monitoring the student's progress and can help to provide pointers for motivating the learner.

Develop a motivating IEP by personalizing it – ask students the following questions:

Reading	Spelling
• Do you enjoy reading?	• Are you a confident speller?
• What sort of things do you like to read?	• If not, which words do you find difficult?
• Are you confident reading aloud in class?	• How do you go about learning new words?

Writing	Mathematics
• Do you like writing?	• Do you like maths?
• Can you write down what you want to say on paper?	• Can you remember tables and number facts easily?
• Is your writing neat?	• Do you get anxious in maths lessons?

From this, you will get information that can be used in the development of the IEP. Then obtain some information on how they perceive themselves as learners by asking them questions about their learning:

- List four things that help you to work well.

- How well organized are you for learning?

- When do you learn better?

- Tell me about your strengths. . . .

- How do you motivate yourself?

- What are your own learning goals?

- Who could be there to help you achieve these goals?

Make motivation intrinsic

Anyone who stops learning is old whether twenty or eighty.

Henry Ford

Ideally, motivation should be intrinsic as this will help the learner become self-motivating. To achieve this, the learner needs to have a goal and some intrinsic determination to succeed. Some students who experience repeated failure can easily become demotivated. This state is often referred to as 'learned helplessness'. It is crucial that the learner does not reach this level and for that reason early success is important when tackling new tasks. It is also important that both extrinsic (rewards) and intrinsic (self-motivation) are taken into account in the planning of learning. Intrinsic motivation can, however, help students take control over their learning.

For intrinsic motivation students need to:

● understand what they are learning

● be inquisitive

● be able to see new learning as part of a bigger picture which can be more motivating

● enjoy the learning experience

● have an appetite for learning.

To begin with, extrinsic motivation can be used in order to engage the student but every effort should be made to shift this gradually to intrinsic motivation.

Develop a questionnaire to help students discover their own learning goals. This type of questionnaire is more effective if given orally just after a talk or a lesson. Some younger students may need some prompting so that it can form the basis of an individual discussion after a lesson. Below are some questions you may want to include:

1. What was my teacher talking about?

2. Some questions that can help me understand the lesson better.

    a. _____

    b. _____

    c. _____

3. What have I got to do now?

4. Do I need any other information?

5. How well can I work on my own now?

This type of discussion with the students will empower them to work independently and assure both the teacher and the students that the students understand the task.

My learning plan and learning goals	
Plan	Goals

Encourage creativity

The art of creativity is making the illogical, logical.

It is interesting to reflect on the fact that many students can only develop their creativity after they leave school. Many, in fact, may fail at school. The examination system often does not reward creativity. The pace of learning seems to prioritize the content and ensures that all examinable areas of the curriculum are covered. This means that there may be less scope for digressing and for encouraging creativity. For many learners, creativity is the principal motivating factor. To encourage creativity it is important to consider the learning styles of the student. It is also important to encourage students' responsibility as this can help students take control over learning and encourage them to use their own ideas.

Anyone can be creative – certainly some students will find creativity easier than others but with encouragement and opportunity every student has the potential to create something that is their own and unique. This is the essence of creativity – to put a stamp of individuality on whatever it is you are working on. This can be seen in montages developed by very young children – when you ask them why they did certain things in a certain way they always have some answer that you might not have thought of – to you it may seem illogical but the art of creativity is making the illogical logical – it is surprising how children can do that.

Game activities are excellent to encourage creativity. Word games, such as brainstorming, where you have to think of many different uses for an object can be a great way for students to show their creativity. For example, uses of a teaspoon, a ball of wool, a hockey stick and so on. You can also have additional dimensions to this by trying to connect a range of objects that seem to have little in common, such as the list above.

5

Reading and creative writing

Practise blending sounds

Blending is smoothly joining phonemes to make a pronunciation close enough to a word to access the word. In competent readers, blending becomes an automated skill. This helps to provide the reading fluency needed for text comprehension. For some readers, however, and particularly beginning readers blending needs practice and tuition before the different types of sounds (phonemes) and letters (graphemes) can be accessed automatically and blended smoothly.

Blending should begin with simple consonant-vowel-consonant (cvc) words using continuous sounds and then gradually move to more complex patterns such as ccvcc using stop consonants. A continuous sound is a sound the student can hold, such as sssssssss or nnnnnnnn. The following sounds are continuous: f, h, l, m, n, s, v and z. Some of these phonograms can also occur in blends making them continuous blends such as sm, sn or pl. All of the short vowel sounds are continuous and so they are easily blended into the final consonant or consonant blend. In a **consonant blend** two or three consonants are smoothly blended together, each consonant sound may be heard in the blend and it may occur at the beginning or end of a word. Some examples of beginning consonant blends are: **bl**‑‑‑ black, **cl**‑‑‑ clap, **spl**‑‑‑ splat, **sn**‑‑‑ snip, **sm**‑‑‑ smash, **br**‑‑‑ brick. Examples of final consonant blends are: **mp**‑‑‑ jump, **nd**‑‑‑ hand, **lt**‑‑‑ felt. In an effort to move from simple to complex, it is best to begin with continuous sounds as opposed to stop sounds as the sound can be held and smoothly blended into the vowel. Eventually, students will be able to blend syllables rather than phonograms.

sm		nd
h	a	p
n	e	t
pl	o	ck

Provide students with different types of blending exercises for both nonsense and real word reading. For a beginning reader, start with torpedo drills using sounds known to the student. In a torpedo blending drill the letters are spaced apart beginning with continuous sounds in the left column, short vowels in the middle column and final consonants in the third column. It is important to have the student hold one sound and smoothly blend it into the next sound that is easiest when using continuous sounds. It is important to have the student synthesize the sounds by voicing what 'word' they made. The goal is to blend and synthesize but not to create or search for real words. It is just as beneficial and maybe more fun to identify nonsense words.

From torpedo drills the student can progress to blending wheels and tachistoscopes that are great for word families, syllables and affixes. All blending exercises should be created using sounds the student has previously learned.

Encourage inferential reading

Inferential reading refers to looking for inferences when reading. It is sometimes referred to as 'reading between the lines'. Inferential reading leads to inferential comprehension, which is a synthesis of information the reader obtains from clues in the text (literal content), intuition, personal knowledge and imagination.

A student may be asked to infer a sequence of events where they are asked what action or incident may have happened between two explicitly stated incidents. They may be asked to describe the nature of a character based on clues in the story or the motives of characters and their relationship with others.

Inferential questioning would include questions such as: What do you think will happen next? Why do you think he said what he did? How do you think . . . ? What kind of person was . . . ? Why did . . . happen?

Although this is a higher-level skill, it needs to be practiced with younger children as well as students further up in school. It helps the reader develop insights into the text and provides a deeper sense of understanding. Many students tend to read at a literal level and may not be able to note the insights that can be obtained from inferences. It is important to ensure that inferences are taught even with students who find reading text challenging.

Some key considerations on teaching inferences relate to encouraging active reading to help the student make sense of the text, monitoring one's own comprehension and resolving misunderstanding as one is reading.

Modelling how to make inferences to students can be an effective way of strengthening a student's own ability to make inferences. Initially asking the questions and leading a discussion are the responsibility of the teachers but with consistent modelling and encouragement, the student will gain confidence in themselves and their ability to know how and when to ask questions themselves. Teachers can model how they themselves draw inferences by:

- thinking aloud their thoughts as they read to pupils

- asking and answering questions that show how they monitor their own comprehension

- making their own thinking processes explicit.

It is important, after modelling, to provide students with ample opportunity to practise as, for many, drawing inferences is more challenging than literal comprehension. This can be done in many ways that are quick but effective.

- Discuss how people make inferences in everyday situations.

- Choose an article and write down sentences that are either facts from the story or inferences. If the sentences are facts they can mark them in one colour, and if the sentences are inferences use a different colour. Have students highlight the passage in the article that shows why their selections are correct.

- Choose a short movie clip and discuss with the students what could be inferred from the clip.

These quick exercises help to develop the skills in using inferences that can then be transferred to reading.

Encourage critical comprehension in reading

Quite a number of children can read fluently but may not be fully accessing the deeper meaning of the text. It is through deeper levels of processing that enhanced comprehension can be achieved. A critical level of comprehension encourages reflection and asks the student to evaluate or make a judgement about the reading. Teachers can facilitate critical comprehension by asking key questions that foster student reflection such as: What did you enjoy about the book? Was there anything you found confusing about the book? Was the plot easy to follow – why/why not? What do you think the author was trying to tell the reader by . . . ? Did you like the way the author described the setting? What could have been done to create a better picture for you? Was this a believable . . . ? Has the information in the text been distorted or over simplified? Is there any reason to doubt . . . ?

Asking questions that encourage critical comprehension allows the student to have some personal ownership over the passage and facilitates insights and opinions. These can help strengthen overall comprehension, retention and recall. To maximize opportunity for the student, it may be more effective to look at many short passages involving real-life experiences rather than focus on a novel or longer story when you are working on strengthening critical comprehension skills.

Propaganda can be an effective way of encouraging students to use critical comprehension skills. Give students a variety of advertisements in different media and ask them to identify the target audience, to pick out the words that hold emotion and to identify what it is that is being 'sold'. How is the advertisement influencing or manipulating the audience? Is it effective? What would make it more or less effective? Are there facts missing? Is the information true and accurate? Will people react emotionally or rationally to this advertisement? (Discuss the propaganda techniques that have been used.)

Another idea for encouraging critical comprehension is to give the students a product, the target audience and a list of criteria. Ask them to brainstorm facts that could be included in an advertisement about the product. Then have them create a leaflet or poster, which would encourage people to buy this product.

For example, have the student create an advirtisement for a new soft drink. Ask them to name it, describe it, create a label and then design a poster to advertise the new product.

Students could also watch or listen to a commercial and then brainstorm ideas for why it is or why it is not effective. It may be useful to have them compare a piece of propaganda with a news item and ask them to list the key differences between the two. They could also compare and contrast a variety of news headlines.

Using critical comprehension skills in the activities given above can be useful not only in the development of these skills but they can also be fun.

Encourage creative thinking

Think outside the box

Creative thinking can provide the learner with opportunities to develop their own style of reflecting and presenting information. It can also release the learner from the restrictions of following a process or sequence, perhaps suggested by the teacher or the textbook. Creative thinking for many learners can be a liberating experience. For some learners this freedom to think creatively can be fun and invigorating and provide a vehicle for emotional expression.

In terms of developing learning skills, creative thinking can promote independent learning. It is also important to acknowledge the self-confidence that can come with independence in learning. Thinking independently and creatively can also help students appreciate other perspectives particularly if they are involved in a role-play activity. It can be surprising to see how motivated some students are when they are given a free reign and allowed to think 'outside the box'. At the same time, many students will need to be supported in developing their creative thinking skills. This can be done by providing an intriguing first sentence to a piece of work and the students have to finish the paragraph. Other activities to promote creative thinking are shown in the following page. One important consideration in relation to creative thinking is that sufficient time must be allowed for the activity. Thinking 'outside the box' takes time as the student often considers additional aspects that may seem unrelated to the problem. This type of tangential thinking can require more processing time and perhaps more drafts of the final response.

Providing structured activities can actually help students to develop their creative thinking skills. Some ideas include:

- Provide a story without an ending to the students and ask them to finish the story using their own ending. This can be a useful group activity. The topic of the story could be, 'no one could even guess what would happen next'. They can then be asked to finish the story.

- Give an article or story without a title, and individual students or a group need to suggest an unusual title for the story.

- Suggest that students draw a picture, but suggest a place to start such as 'draw a ranch'. Then they can, one-step at a time, add to the picture by going through a list of questions that pertain to the ranch such as: Is there a house? Is there a barn? What type of animals are there, do any people live on the ranch, is there a lake or pond on the ranch, what types of activities take place? What is the weather like? How do people get to and from the ranch? These questions, given one at a time, can help the student develop a picture of the scene without it feeling overwhelming. From here, you can create all sorts of writing activities such as: write a story of something that happened on your ranch, write a descriptive paragraph about your ranch, describe one of the characters on your ranch, have your character send a postcard from your ranch etc.

- Draw a photo of a made-up character which could be human or animal. Encourage the students to use colour and add a lot of detail. Then ask the students to write a descriptive paragraph describing the character, their friends, favourite things to eat, activities they enjoy etc.

- Working in groups, each student should write a phrase about anything at all and see if all the phrases can be joined together to make a story – they can use other phrases and join them together but they must include all the phrases suggested by each member of the group.

Develop reading goals

Learning will be more effective if you have a goal in mind when you are reading with a student or having a student read aloud.

Possible reading goals:

- Fluency: involves the rate of reading as well as the ability to read connected text smoothly, accurately and automatically with voiced expression and comprehension.

- Comprehension: the level of understanding one has after reading a passage.

- Word attack: the ability to convert graphemes into phonemes.

- Punctuation: stopping at and acknowledging punctuation through voiced expression when reading. Often, students who struggle with punctuation will read to the end of the line rather than taking a breath when they reach the punctuation.

- Intonation: the variation in the voice when reading aloud.

- Voiced Expression: reading without voiced expression can indicate lack of understanding. Ask yourself if the student is reading in a monotone or if their voice is too loud or too soft

- Postural Habits: take note of how the student handles the book as well as the position they sit in. Is their body strained or tense, do they hold the book too close or too far away? Is the book floppy in their hands, do they drop it frequently or loose their page?

Choose an approach to reading that is reflective of your reading goal. For example, if your goal is:

- Fluency: choose a book that is slightly below the student's reading level or one that the student has read or heard before. Paired reading[1] is an approach that works well when working on improving reading fluency.

- Comprehension: teacher and student take turns in thinking aloud and asking questions at each level of comprehension (critical, creative, literal, inferential). Reciprocal reading[2] is an approach that works well for strengthening reading comprehension skills.

- Word attack: immediately prior to the reading, give a list of vocabulary from the text that you think the student may struggle with. Write these words or phrases on cards for the student to read. This way, when the student sees them in the reading, he/she will be familiar.

- Punctuation: tap at the end of each sentence when the student reaches a period, question mark or exclamation mark. This will draw their attention to the punctuation and eventually they will pause and wait for the tap. The student can also be encouraged to take over the tapping.

- Intonation: using poetry or text with dialogue will help with this skill.

- Voiced expression: reading of plays or other readings with many dialogues having quotations are very useful for encouraging voiced expression.

- Postural habits: let the student handle the book after good modelling.

---

1 Paired reading: a reading approach involving the parent/teacher and the child (see Topping, 2001). It is a structured systemic approach that follows a series of steps involving the parent/teacher and the child reading aloud together.
2 Reciprocal reading: this involves extended question and answer discussions between the parent/teacher and the child throughout the reading of text thus helping to develop a deeper understanding.

Selecting books for students

Appropriate selection of a book is crucial to stimulate reading and to sustain motivation for reading. Children, when selecting a book, are actually thinking, evaluating and may be using some critical learning skills such as making judgements and formulating opinions through the process of book selection. There is a wide range of criteria that may or may not be appropriate for every student but the following can act as a general guide:

- Title – is the title of the book catchy and meaningful?

- Use of language in the book – avoid confusing vocabulary and long words.

- Presentation – is the size and type of font, front cover, visuals, length of the chapters of the book presentable?

- Index at the end – is there an index with vocabulary provided in the book?

- What is the interest level of the student?

- Is there an audio and/or video version available to the student?

- Is there an abridged version of the book?

- Are there any teacher's notes for the book?

A reading log is a great place for students to keep track of the titles and authors they have read as well as recording their reactions to the text. You can create your own list of criteria to record. The chart given below is only a suggestion.

My reading log			Date: _____
Title	Author	Type of reading	My thoughts on the book. Did I like it?
1.			
2.			
3.			
4.			
5.			

This type of chart can be used in many different ways. You may want to use it as a motivational chart to keep track of books over vacation periods. You may want to use it as an expanded exercise where the students can first record the books they read with a brief description and then organize the list from most recommended to those they wouldn't recommend and why. The students could then present their list to the class and share their opinion of why others should read it or not.

Use art and visuals for creative writing

Students who may have difficulty coming up with ideas for writing may be more successful if they begin with an activity that leads to writing. Often, the difficulty is in coming up with the ideas and so it can be very useful if the activity is more concrete. It may also be useful to make the activity very structured, but allow for flexibility within the structure. You can begin with an art activity by asking the students to create something and then design a series of writing activities around the student's creation. For example, students can create a number of three-dimensional characters and then when they are finished with the models they can be asked to write a series of stories based on these characters. Join a few of the characters together with others in the class and they can then start creating stories about the characters that perhaps describes some sort of newsworthy event, good or bad. The idea is to make the activity of writing more alive and more real and this can be done through art and the use of craft materials. There are a number of different ideas and tasks that can stem from this. One such idea is to produce a newspaper using the stories from the class. This is developed on the next page.

Have the students work together as a class to develop and produce a newspaper based on the characters they created themselves (see previous page). Begin by having the students come up with all of the different types of columns in a newspaper – news, features, adverts, entertainment, classified advertisements, sport, cartoons, kids corner etc – and then have them decide which will be appropriate for their newspaper.

Choose groups of two or three students to take a section each and they have to be responsible for that part of the newspaper. Appoint an editor, a deputy editor and a photographer for the newspaper. Everyone else will be reporters and have to develop the stories into articles or advertisements. You can have the class photographer photograph the characters the students created as well as the editor, deputy editor and journalists (students).

The articles will of course be ficticious but you can encourage the students to look at a local newpaper for story ideas. It could be fun to have a cartoon strip as well as an advice column where one student writes a letter from a character with a problem and the letter (and the problem) is answered by another character. This is the type of activity where different learners can all come together because there are so many possibilities within the project.

You can also have a 'reader's letters' page and get the class to write individual letters to the editor about some community topic and provide a prize for the winning letter.

Use prompts for creative writing

For many students creative writing can present a real challenge. Often they have difficulty in actually getting started. This can in fact be the toughest part of the creative writing process. This difficulty can be overcome by using prompts as well as providing structure words that can help to inspire, expand and develop story lines.

A prompt can be a keyword, a story line, a title, the first sentence in a story an event that can be developed into a story or a description of an event that the writer has to put into context and expand on. Prompts may get the story started but students will need guidance to sustain the story. This is where writing frames can be useful as they can help to develop story lines but the prompt is necessary to generate the initial thoughts on the story.

Some prompts can include the following:

- Close your eyes and describe an object in the room.

- Find an old picture from a book or an art gallery and write about the people in it and the type of life you think they experienced.

- Select four words randomly from the dictionary and see if you can use these words in a story.

- Choose a poem that you like and take one of the lines from the poem as the opener to your story.

- Write about a weird day at school.

- Write what you would do with three wishes.

- Write about your first toy – or at least the one you can remember most vividly.

- Begin the story with the phrase 'I wish someone would have told me'.

You can build up a bank of prompts and get the students themselves to compile a list of prompts as they find that quite a fun activity.

Develop a matrix with numbers such as:

1	2	3	4	5
6	7	8	9	10
11	12	13	14	15
16	17	18	19	20
21	22	23	24	25

Write out 25 prompts under the numbers (1-25) in the matrix. If you have a pocket chart in the classroom you can write the prompts on paper and insert one prompt into each pocket. The students would then go and choose a prompt from the pocket chart.

Using the matrix, have the students choose (or assign them) numbers from 1-25 until each student has a number. The students would then go and choose a prompt from the pocket chart. Once they have finished their story they can choose another number and begin the process again with a new prompt and a new story.

The matrix shown provides a few examples of prompts to get started.

1	2	3	4	5
I wish someone would have told me...	It was the weirdest day....	If I could have any pet I wanted, I would choose a...	Yesterday at the pond my friends ...	I am sorry I was late today but ....

Provide a comfortable place for students to read

Reading while sitting on a hard chair in the library may not be preferable for most of the students. Try to make reading as pleasurable as possible by providing some choice in where the students sit when reading. It may be necessary to make the seating arrangements as comfortable as they can be. Some factors that can be considered include: type of chairs, lighting, seating arrangement – in groups or individually, length of time for reading, time of day, students' individual preferences of reading materials and environment.

Beanbags are very popular with many children when reading. They can be comfortable and informal and for some children, particularly those with reading difficulties, it can remove some of the stress from the reading activity. They are available in many fabrics including leather which is durable or vinyl which can be easily wiped off.

Another way to create a cozy and inviting reading area is to lay out a plush carpet and line it with several big, soft cushions as well as a few smaller ones. The idea is to provide an area students will gravitate to and want to stay in. You could ask students to remove their shoes and encourage them to curl up or stretch out, getting into a comfortable reading position.

Creating an environment free of distractions that is cosy and comfortable where children can recline and put their feet up can encourage the quiet, calm and relaxed behaviour that is necessary for meaningful reading. An enclosed quiet area is easy to create with a room divider that could be a bookshelf, a curtain or a movable, freestanding divider. Putting a soft, plush carpet in the area with a selection of several big cushiony pillows will provide a place to sit and a place to lean back on. Carpets with pillows can be economical, easily rolled up and stored if the space is needed for something else and can be cleaned regularly.

For younger children, a reading tent is a good idea. It is important that comfort and potential distractions are considered. A reading tent can reduce distractions and still provide both novelty and comfort.

It is important to find out what each individual student prefers and to try, as far as possible, to provide this for the student. If it is not possible to do this at school, it is still a useful exercise as the student can be encouraged to use his/her preferences at home when reading.

Key points to consider for the individual student:

- **Lighting**. Check the lighting there. Is it adequate? You should be able to see the page without strain. Does the light create a glare?

- **Ventilation and temperature**. Stuffy rooms put you to sleep. You should have plenty of fresh air and the temperature should be comfortable.

- **Reading position**. An uncomfortable position can create a strain that results in fatigue. But if you are too comfortable, you read yourself to sleep. The ideal is a balance between the two but the key is that the reader should feel at ease and relaxed when reading.

- **Distractions.** If you sit near a door or window, every movement will claim your attention. If you have a radio on, your concentration may wander from book to sound. Reading with the television on in the background will cause distractions.

Expand vocabulary

Many students have difficulty with writing because they cannot access the words they need and may have difficulty using a dictionary. It is important, therefore, to teach dictionary skills and these are highlighted in the following page. It is also a good idea to provide students with a list of keywords that they may want to use in a piece of writing. These words can be divided into different categories such as descriptive words, names, places, 'feeling' words etc.

To begin with, you can give the student a passage with some words missing (cloze passage) and get them to fill in the blanks. To help students with this, some words can be placed at the top of the page and they have to select the words from this list.

It may be necessary to provide many different types of activities to encourage students to expand their vocabulary. Some students may enjoy receiving a 'word of the day'. They can be encouraged to learn the meaning of the new word and then be challenged to try to use the word as many times as possible that day.

Many students will need to be explicitly taught how to use a dictionary (and thesaurus). Begin by sequencing the alphabet in order to strengthen the student's ability and speed in looking up words in a thesaurus and dictionary. Give them exercises where they have to give the sequence of just three letters such as 'what are the two letters that come after "j". They may need a lot of practice with this first step.

Next, teach the use of guide words – first and last word on a page – and give them exercises encouraging the students to practise using guide words. For example, create a page with guide words along with a list of words that would be found on the same page as the guide words and some words that could come before or after.

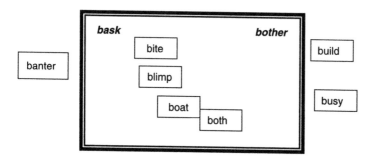

Look at the following list of words: banter, build, blimp, both, bite, busy, boat. If the guide words are bask and bother, will they be found between bask and bother (thus being on the same page) or will they come before or after.

Creating and using a personal word bank

Many readers have difficulty in writing fluently because they have a word finding difficulty or they have a limited vocabulary. Additionally, some students may use the wrong word or use the word in the wrong context. It is useful to provide a list of keywords but, additionally, it is a good idea if the student created his/her own words. This can be done through the development of a word bank that is personalized for the student. It is also a good idea to have the meaning of the word next to the word to ensure that the word is used appropriately. Most software programmes have a good thesaurus that can also be used for this purpose and the student can use this to add to his/her personal word bank.

Building a Word Bank

Give the students a topic for writing a story along with a few keywords. Before the students begin to write, they can create their own personal word bank to use in the story by looking up the keywords in a thesaurus. For example, give the students the topic 'pirates' and then give them the words ocean, treasure, boat and shipwrecked. They can also brainstorm for other words that trigger their imagination when they hear the word 'pirate'. Using a children's thesaurus, have the students look up each word and build a bank of words to use in a story. Then using their bank of words they can begin to create a storyline using vocabulary that is more interesting than they may have been able to come up with without the word bank.

Another way to get students using a thesaurus and adding to their word bank is to give them a common word in the middle of a page. Using a thesaurus, have the students fill up the page with words that could be used instead of the common word. Some common words that tend to be overused in students writing are: said, happy, sad, cold, hot, great, fantastic, amazing, mad, pretty.

They can keep all of their personal word banks in a notebook for future writing.

6 Successful learning

Use peer interaction to develop learning competencies

It is important to encourage students to work together constructively to develop their learning skills. They need to appreciate that learning is something they **can** have control over. It does not just happen – they can make it happen. This can be done through working together and they need to be encouraged to reflect on the learning processes they are engaged in. Too often, students are preoccupied with the result and the end product but it is important to get them to engage in the process of learning and to share in each other's skills and abilities. This process of peer interaction can be made more effective by providing students with a framework for questioning so that they know whether they are on the right track or not, and very importantly which questions to ask of each other. The idea behind this is that it provides the group with reflective skills and encourages them to respect each other's ideas and styles. It may be necessary as a teacher to reflect on the group dynamics. Either group the students with similar learning styles to make the collaborative process smoother or mix different styles within the group ensuring the styles complement each other. It is important that students do get practice working with others for different styles. Peer interaction can be a useful way of encouraging students to reflect on their own learning style and to appreciate other students learning preferences.

It is important to have a range of strategies and techniques to assist with successful learning. Demonstrate these to students and allow them to become proficient at using the ones they like to use.

Provide a 4-point group framework for questioning during a group task.

1. What have we got to do here?

This encourages the learners to reflect on the task. Too many students rush into a task and then realize midway through that they have not fully understood the question. This allows them to analyse the task and provides the opportunity to plan a response.

2. What is each person in the group responsible for?

Who is good at leading the discussion, taking notes, reflecting and asking the questions, finding the resources, doing the visuals, organizing the information, presenting the information, reporting on the output.

3. What is our plan for completing this task?

Identify the beginning, middle and end part of the task, allocating how long each part of the task will take, giving the group some control over the process.

4. Reflective meeting

At the end of the project/task the group should have an open discussion on how well they did, what they may have done differently and what they learned from doing the task both as individuals and as a group.

Time management

There is always more information and tasks to complete than students have time for. Everyone has to practise time management. It is important to discuss this with students – even young students – as it is never too early to help students organize how they plan to use their time. You might want to keep these 6 steps to time management in mind.

1. **Wanting** to use time more efficiently is the motivation part and is really very important as the student has to be organized and has to use his/her time efficiently.

2. **Planning** what needs to be done will need practice and you could start by giving the student a template of a plan and get them to complete it.

3. **Organizing** what needs to be done will involve making a 'To do' list – using colour and patterns can make it a fun activity for students.

4. **Doing** what needs to be done is the action part and the student may need some initial support with this.

5. **Self-monitoring** what is being done is important for developing independent learning.

6. **Evaluating** what has been done can help to make learning more efficient and help the student to be able to use effective strategies for new learning.

All the way through the learning process, students should be encouraged to ask themselves questions such as how can I do this more effectively and how can I use my time more efficiently.

Get students to follow the routine below:

- Write down tasks as they are received including due dates.
- Construct a weekly list based on order of importance.
- Allocate tasks to appropriate time slots during the week; encourage students to consider their personal activity schedule when thinking of due dates.
- Undertake more thought-orientated tasks at times when freshest.
- Divide long tasks into smaller units allocating time for each.
- Look for tasks that can be discarded.
- Identify sources that can enable successful completion of tasks.
- Avoid taking on more than is reasonably possible to complete.
- Checking off tasks once they are completed is an important part of the process as this gives them self-satisfaction.

To Do:

	Time	Task	Completed
Monday	_____	_____	☐
Tuesday	_____	_____	☐
Wednesday	_____	_____	☐
Thursday	_____	_____	☐
Friday	_____	_____	☐
Saturday	_____	_____	☐
Sunday	_____	_____	☐

Maths strategies

Students can often experience difficulties in maths even though they are competent in other subjects. These difficulties can include memory, speed of working, literacy and understanding diagrams and graphs. Some students are also challenged because of their lack of conceptual understanding in maths and understanding the very specific meaning of mathematical terms, which can also be confused with everyday non-mathematical meanings. Weak understanding of mathematical concepts plus an uncertainty about procedures and methods can result in a lack of confidence in writing tasks, for example, explaining, discussing, working out and making notes.

Some students are able to cope by following instructions during the lesson, but when they try the same procedure for homework, they have forgotten what to do. Often transferring their own notes on to index cards with examples can help them to remember the procedure in further problems. If the index cards are filed under the topic heading then they are easily located for future reference.

Develop a chart such as the one below with a column for difficulties and one for response. Support the student in developing one of their own that they can keep adding to it. An example is shown below.

Difficulty	Response
Difficulty with mathematical language, e.g. horizontal, vertical, diagonal	Use floor mats or carpet tiles arranged in a square and allow students to make a diagonal line corner to corner
Verbal instructions are forgotten quickly	Give instructions one step at a time. Chunk information. Encourage the student to highlight each step in a written maths problem
May forget a long sequence of steps	Develop a sequence checklist for calculation methods and procedures
Difficulties with remembering the sequence of times tables	Teach times tables in a multi-sensory way looking for patterns, using colour coding, verbalizing using rhythm and rhyme, finger tables and listening to tables with music
Difficulty remembering formulae	Teach formulae in a fun way. Use mnemonics and rhymes, colour coding and jingles
Unable to remember details of the homework	Give out the homework at the beginning of the lesson when there is time to check that the student has all the information
	Allow the student extra time and ensure that he/she is not under pressure to read and respond quickly

Many mathematical terms are multi-syllabic, for example, isosceles, vertices, multiplication; for some students it can be difficult to read fluently. Also, in maths text, the flow of reading is not always left to right as some questions contain tables and diagrams. It can be important to check the readability level of the maths books.

Use multiple intelligences

There has been a great deal of discussion on the value of the concept of intelligence and the work of Howard Gardner on multiple intelligences. Multiple intelligences can help to gain an understanding of the student's different learning preferences and can provide some guidance on how to develop materials and teach a wide range of students. Practical applications of these intelligences should be explored when teaching students. Gardner believes each individual has 8 intelligences. These are:

1. Visual/spatial intelligence

2. Verbal/linguistic intelligence

3. Logical/mathematical intelligence

4. Bodily/Kinaesthetic intelligence

5. Musical/rhythmic intelligence

6. Interpersonal intelligence (social skills)

7. Intrapersonal intelligence (metacognitive skills)

8. Naturalistic intelligence (awareness of surroundings and of nature).

Make up a chart inserting some practical applications for each of the multiple intelligences – as in the example below:

Intelligence type	Characteristics	Practical applications
Visual/spatial intelligence	Puzzle building, understanding charts and graphs, sketching, painting, constructing, designing practical objects	Designing and producing a folio of creative and visual product
Verbal/linguistic intelligence	Listening, speaking, writing, explaining	Explaining concepts or answers to questions without writing it down
Logical/ mathematical intelligence	Ability to use reason, logic and numbers, performing complex mathematical calculations, working with geometric shapes	Use formulae and shapes as well as whole page diagrams and flow charts
Bodily/Kinaesthetic intelligence	These learners express themselves through movement. Experiencing the physical process of a task enables them to remember and process information	Hands-on experience of practical tasks will provide excellent ways in which to remember information
Musical/rhythmic intelligence	Whistling, playing musical instruments, recognizing tonal patterns, composing music, remembering melodies, understanding the structure and rhythm of music	When memorizing information, the use of a poem/rap to do this can help jog the memory in an exam

Interpersonal intelligence	Seeing things from other perspectives (dual perspective), cooperating with groups, noticing people's moods, motivations and intentions	Group discussion, arguments and debates
Intrapersonal intelligence	These learners try to understand their inner feelings, strengths and weaknesses	Evaluating work, developing learning strategies – group work
Naturalistic intelligence	Studying in a natural setting, learning about how things work. Categorizing, preservation and conservation	Look at connections in nature and life cycles

Whole school approaches

Promote emotional literacy

Emotional literacy is important as it helps learners feel more aware of their needs and the needs of others and it can help with collaborative learning. Emotional literacy can be linked to emotional intelligence. Both relate to the capacity in individuals (and groups) to perceive, understand and mange emotions in oneself and relating to others. This is very important for individual and social learning. Emotional literacy, to have any impact on the education and the lives of children, has to be fully absorbed and fully included into a whole school ethos. This is important as it is often the case that emotional problems underlie the behavioural problems that can be seen in the classroom.

There are five pathways to emotional intelligence – self-awareness, self-regulation, motivation, empathy and social competence. These are all necessary for the development of emotional well-being and emotional literacy. To ensure that schools have an ethos that is conducive to emotional literacy, factors such as organizational climate, organizational change, bullying, teacher stress, circle time, communication, motivation, feedback, thinking skills, developing interpersonal skills and the role of reflection are all crucial.

You can help to develop emotional literacy by preparing an emotional literacy checklist. An example of this is shown below.

- Does the learner show any stress signs?

- Can the student be left to work independently?

- Can the student persist with the task or will he/she require monitoring?

- Can the learner only work for short periods?

- Does the learner require constant reassurance?

- Is the learner aware of the needs of others?

The above can serve as a monitoring or checking sheet to ascertain that the learner is emotionally ready for the task. It may be necessary to do some preparatory work on learner's emotional well-being before they can work independently on tasks. It is also worth noting that emotional literacy is a whole school responsibility. Children may well develop emotional literacy in one class, but if they are in a school which does not have an emotional literacy ethos then the gains will be lost. The idea of developing a sound emotional and social ethos should be one of the school's priorities

Becoming emotionally prepared for the task

It is worthwhile taking time to ensure the learner is emotionally ready for the task. Some learners can feel totally swamped and overwhelmed by a task and it is necessary to talk this through with them before they proceed.

They may have difficulty in accessing the learning materials and this can provide a reason why some learners stumble emotionally when learning – perhaps the books and other materials they need are beyond their current level of knowledge and understanding. This needs to be checked out with the learner.

To ascertain readiness it is important to check out some points before the task such as: Can the student identify the key points of the topic? The key points should be discussed with the student individually and new information should be identified before the student embarks on the task.

At the end of the task learners should be asked if they think they were successful and what they found easy or difficult. But importantly, they should be asked what could/should they have known before they started the task? This question is important as it relates to how prepared they were for the task.

Although these points relate to individual students and are carried out in the classroom they should be considered as whole school approaches as they represent good practice which will benefit all students.

Double F, P, R formula

Use the double F, P, R formula

(Feelings, Feedback, Perspective, Process, Reasons, Realign)

Feelings – ask how they feel about doing the task.

It is important to ensure that the child has a positive view of the task – any barrier that prevents that should be dealt with at this stage.

Feedback – feedback to them what they have already achieved towards doing the task.

This is important as it reassures the students and helps them appreciate that the goal is achievable.

Perspective – put in perspective what they have to achieve.

Process – together with the learner talk through the process – indicate clearly what has to be done first and then second.

Reasons – identify the reasons for any feelings of being overwhelmed and why this should be the case.

Realign – this is about goals and expectations – realign jointly with the learners some suggested goals that can be achieved.

It is important to go through each of these individually with the student.

This process also provides a degree of control for the learner, particularly the last part where they can devise their own goals for the new learning. It is important that all new learnings are within the leaner's comfort zone; therefore, it is crucial that they have some input in devising their goals. There is a great deal of research on the importance of emotional factors in learners and it is worthwhile spending some time in ensuring that the child is emotionally prepared for the new piece of learning. This may require some pre-task discussion or a boost to their confidence. This can come from ensuring that the task is appropriate. Therefore, getting the child to be emotionally prepared for learning can have as much to do with the task as the child.

De-stress the school

It is important to consider the relationship between stress and learning. There is a wide range of reasons why learners can experience stress. This includes:

- Worry/anxiety

It is important to be aware that children can worry about things that seem to be irrelevant to the adult. It is important to take all children's anxieties seriously.

- Social reasons

School is a social institution but some children find it difficult to fit into school. This can make them socially isolated and can be a chronic source of unhappiness for many children.

- Family reasons

Families can occupy the central role in children's lives. If things go wrong or changes are made to the family life in whatever way, this can have an upsetting affect on some children.

- School learning

School can also be a competitive institution. This is fine as it can stretch children to achieve, but at the same time it can demoralize children who have difficulty in achieving. Ensure expectations are realistic.

- School friendships

Peer-group friendships are vitally important to most children. A breakdown in these can be the main source of unhappiness at school for some children. This should not be taken lightly and activities such as circle time can help to develop peer-group friendships and understanding. Be on the lookout for bullying in school.

Some strategies that can deal with stress and anxiety include the following:

- Activities

Most types of activities can help to alleviate stress. Children often feel more relaxed after exercise as long as the exercise is not of a competitive nature.

- Music

It is important that the right type of music is selected – the best idea is to get the student to try working and studying with different types of music to work out which, if any, is best.

- Yoga

Yoga involves both mental and physical capacities and has a relaxing effect on people as it helps them to switch off from their daily routine and helps them to relax.

- Reflection

Reflection essentially means that children need to take time out from what they are doing to reflect. Reflection can help them to deal with the pace of life in school and the expectations.

- Talk

Talking though a problem or a situation can help to clarify the situation in ones mind.

- Reading

Reading can be relaxing but some children have difficulty in reading, and for them it can be a stressful activity. It is important to try to engage all children in reading, and to do this it is crucial that the right levels of reading materials are found.

- Succeeding

Success can be enjoyed and takes much pressure off an individual. But children may not be successful in every area of school life. It is important that the expectations and the task are geared to the individual child. That way there will be a greater possibility of that child achieving success.

Prioritize effective learning through staff development

Effective learning should be seen as a whole school initiative and therefore should be a priority in staff development.

Some key points that should be considered in staff development include:

- the need for opportunities to help all learners develop social learning skills

- the nature of the learning experience for all learners

- whole school awareness of emotional literacy and stress prevention

- the need to value all students and staff as this will influence the school ethos and the learning performances of all students.

Some of the issues that can have an impact on the staff relate to the multi-faceted dimensions of teachers' roles in schools today. They can experience both role ambiguity and role conflict. Some teachers may be unclear of their actual role – for example, the conflict that often exists between dealing with the learning and emotional needs of the children on the one hand, and the need to get through a crowded syllabus and ensuring that the students are equipped for examinations on the other hand can produce role conflict. Sometimes, conflict can arise due to misunderstandings and the inability to identify the actual problem. For this reason, staff development is important as it involves the whole staff and can provide opportunities to air concerns about the pace and the nature of the students' learning experiences and the staff's teaching role in development work, planning and teaching.

Develop a staff workshop to address whole school needs to enhance effective learning in the school. An outline of the key points is shown below and this is in fact a summary of the key points of this book.

Slide 1	Slide 2
Key factors for effective learning	Learning to learn
<ul><li>Identifying and dealing with barriers to learning</li><li>Learning to learn</li><li>Memory</li><li>Motivation</li><li>Making reading and writing effective</li><li>Successful learning</li><li>Whole school approaches</li></ul>	<ul><li>Make connections</li><li>Metacognition</li><li>Promote independent learning</li><li>Learning styles</li><li>Reduce stress</li><li>Develop collaborative learning</li></ul>
Slide 3	**Slide 4**
Memory Key ideas to develop memory skills	Motivation
<ul><li>Prioritize</li><li>Organize information</li><li>Use visuals</li><li>Chunking and making connections</li><li>Re-enact and discuss</li></ul>	<ul><li>Stimulate to motivate</li><li>Locus of control/intrinsic motivation</li><li>IEPs and motivation</li><li>Creativity and motivation</li></ul>
Slide 5	**Slide 6**
Reading and effective learning	<ul><li>Writing and effective learning</li><li>Developing creative writing</li><li>Visual planning skills</li><li>Expanding vocabulary</li></ul>
<ul><li>Inferential reading and critical thinking</li><li>Develop reading goals</li><li>Selecting a book</li><li>Provide vocabulary lists</li><li>The reading environment</li></ul>	

Slide 7	Slide 8
Successful learning	Whole school approaches
• Developing learning competencies	• Emotional literacy
• Help students to use self-questioning	• Self-esteem
• The importance of time management	• School factors – ethos, stress
• Maths and effective learning	• Staff development
• Multiple intelligence and successful learning	• The school environment – a positive learning environment

Further reading and other sources of information

Books and toolkits

Came, F., Cooke, G. and Brough, M. (2002), *Learning Toolkit volume 1 and volume 2* available at Learning Works, 9 Barrow Close, Marlborough, Wiltshire, SN8 2YY.

www.learning-works.org.uk

Ginnis, P. (2003), *The Teacher's Toolkit – Raise Classroom Achievement with Strategies for Every Learner*. Carmarthen, Wales: Crown House Publishing Ltd.

www.crownhouse.co.uk

This teacher's toolkit contains ideas and game activities for teaching and learning.

Lazear, D. (2004), *OutSmart Yourself! 16 Proven Multiple Intelligence Strategies for Becoming Smarter Than You Think You Are.*

This book focuses on the theory of multiple intelligences proposed by Harvard psychologist Dr Howard Gardner.

David Lazear Products available at www.davidlazear.com and Arlington Heights, IL, Skylight Professional Development.

Reid, G. (2007), *Motivating Learners in the Classroom: Ideas and Strategies*. London: Sage Publications.

www.drgavinreid.com

Reid, G. (2007), Learning Styles and Inclusion. London: Sage Publications.

Topping, K. J. (2001), *Thinking Reading Writing: A Practical Guide to Paired Learning with Peers, Parents and Volunteers*. New York and London: Continuum International.

Vygotsky, L. S. (1978), *Mind in Society: The Development of Higher Psychological Processes*. Cambridge, MA: Harvard University Press.

Vygotsky, L. S. (1986), *Thought and Language*. Cambridge, MA: MIT Press.

Other sources of information

Alistair Smith number of books on learning including Accelerated Learning: A User's Guide and The ALPS Approach: Accelerated Learning in Primary Schools.

www.alite.co.uk

Accelerated Learning in Training and Education, Alite Ltd., Bourne Park Cores End Road, Bourne End, Buckinghamshire, SL8 5AS, United Kingdom

Barrington Stoke Ltd (10 Belford Terrace, Edinburgh EH4 3DQ; website: www.barringtonstoke.co.uk) provide a range of books for reluctant readers, including teenage fiction.

Crossbow Education (41 Sawpit Lane, Brocton, Stafford ST17 0TE; tel: 01785 660902; website: www.crossboweducation.com) specialize in games for children with difficulties in reading, spelling and memory and produce game activities on literacy and numeracy.

Mandy Appleyard, Educational Consultant, Fun Track Learning Centre, Perth, Western Australia
Centre address, Fun Track Learning Centre, Unit 2, 590 Stirling Highway, Mosman Park WA 6012, Western Australia, www.funtrack.com.au